T0102657

Greasy Creek

Larry W Janis

WestBow
P R E S S
A DIVISION OF THOMAS NELSON

Copyright © 2010 Larry W Janis

All rights reserved. No part of this book may be used or reproduced by any means, graphic, electronic, or mechanical, including photocopying, recording, taping or by any information storage retrieval system without the written permission of the publisher except in the case of brief quotations embodied in critical articles and reviews.

WestBow Press books may be ordered through booksellers or by contacting:

WestBow Press
A Division of Thomas Nelson
1663 Liberty Drive
Bloomington, IN 47403
www.westbowpress.com
1-(866) 928-1240

Because of the dynamic nature of the Internet, any Web addresses or links contained in this book may have changed since publication and may no longer be valid. The views expressed in this work are solely those of the author and do not necessarily reflect the views of the publisher, and the publisher hereby disclaims any responsibility for them.

ABOUT THE COVER:
The picture on the cover of this book is a current picture of what was called the baptizing hole on Greasy Creek when Bud lived there. His father baptized a number of people from both Pine Log and Coffman Baptist Churches. As a fitting footnote to this story Larry Janis' daughter, Susan, was proposed to, and accepted the proposal by Randy Dean at this spot in 2008. The author's wife was able to be a part of the wedding ceremony.

ISBN: 978-1-4497-0451-3 (sc)
ISBN: 978-1-4497-0452-0 (dj)
ISBN: 978-1-4497-0477-3 (e)

Library of Congress Control Number: 2010938091

Printed in the United States of America

WestBow Press rev. date: 9/28/2010

Contents

Memorial

Mrs. Patsy Janis

This book was originally begun as part of a project to meet the requirements for a college course in children's literature. It was finished many years later thanks to the efforts of my late wife Patsy. Due to her work the main part of the book was completed, typed, and survived several moves and fire. During the latter days of her fight with cancer she asked for an envelope from her dresser drawer. She took out a large handful of twenty dollar bills and handed them to me saying these were being saved for a special project but I was to use them for whatever I saw fit. She never told me what that project was, but I believe it was to get this book completed and published. Because the book would not have existed without her, I wish to dedicate it to her memory.

Preface

In writing this book the author has drawn strictly from memory. The places, events, and people are real. The names are authentic although the spelling may not be correct in all cases. These events took place over sixty years ago and the author had to guess at the actual conversations, which took place. The drawings were made by the author and again were from memory and so may not be completely true to actual details. However, they are close enough to give the readers a good idea of what things looked like.

The author has visited some of these places in recent years. A few still look much as they did when he was a boy, while others have changed a great deal. The Clearwater Store and the house he lived in are gone and a bridge has been built over the creek where the story of the flood took place. The creek bed has been altered in places to prevent erosion of the roadbed and the road beside it has been changed so that it no longer fords the creek several times to reach the Boyd's place where it now ends rather than going up to the little town of Avon. Wineries have been built in some of the areas Bud used to walk to school in. However, some of the people are still living in the same places talked about in the book and some of the same buildings have survived.

It should be mentioned that the stories in this book do not begin with Buds first contact with Greasy Creek. He did not expect to one day live down the creek from Avon when his father first preached at the little settlement. They lived many miles away at that time and, since they had no car, had to pay for a taxi, (35¢ for the first quarter mile then 3¢ a mile), to take them on Sunday mornings and either wait until church was over or else return in the evening if they were going to stay all day. In fact, it was on one of those days Bud was to have an unforgettable experience. Bud and his family planned to eat dinner (lunch) with one of the church families and spend the afternoon with them. As they entered the front yard they were greeted by a large, very friendly, black and tan coonhound. The dog stood taller than Bud when on his hind legs. He seemed eager to make this fact clear to Bud as soon as they met. As Bud was trying to pet the excited dog he suddenly began to feel warm and wet from the waist down one of his legs. He looked down to see the dog had mistaken him for a fire hydrant. Bud was so shocked he just stood there not knowing what to do. He had to spend the afternoon wearing a pair of borrowed pants much too large for him. Needless to say, the dog did not become one of his favorites. Buds father often paid more for the taxi trips than he received for preaching but he would go to any church that asked him to come. He never questioned how much they were going to pay him before agreeing to go there. He just accepted whatever they gave him.

Acknowledgements

Because this book would not have been written if I were solely responsible for it, I wish to thank the following people for their help. Besides my wife, I thank my daughter Susan Dean, an old friend R. J. Lievsey, fellow workers Carla Castillo Stuckenschneider, Chad W. Smith, and a former student of mine, Elizabeth Rupp Hoelker.

Chapter 1
Moving Day

Bud was very excited as he helped his parents load the big truck. Today Bud and his family were moving. This was not an ordinary move, from one house to another; Bud was going to move back into the past. At least that's the way it seemed to him. Just think for a moment what it would be like to go back to the way your great grandparents lived. That is what Bud was going to do, and was he ever happy about it.

Several years of Bud's life had been spent on the farm. He certainly was no stranger to country life. But this time, things would be different. In the home they were moving to there would be no electricity, no telephone, no radio, no water faucets, no thermostats, no television, not even a bathroom. What a change it was going to be. Buds' mother and father had grown up under similar conditions so the move was merely going to be a step back to things that were less convenient. However, Bud and his sister were not used to, or familiar with, some of the things they would encounter so it seemed like a great adventure to him. True, there would be a lot more work to do, but work can sometimes be fun, especially when it is something new and different.

At last the big truck was loaded and the driver asked Bud if he would like to ride with him in the cab. Would he? Boy! Would that be fun? He had never ridden in a truck as big as this one. Bud's father told him it would be alright for him to go in the truck and the rest of the family would follow in the car.

For several miles they rolled along on a nice big highway. Then the driver, Mr. Clark, slowed the truck down and signaled that he was going to turn off the highway. The new road they were on was paved but it was much narrower than the big highway. Soon however, the pavement ended, and they were traveling along over a gravel road that was much bumpier. After what seemed a very long time to Bud the truck slowed down and pulled off the road.

"We're going to fill up with gas here Bud, do you want to get out and stretch a bit?"

Bud climbed down from the cab and walked around the truck. He looked up at the big false fronts on the only two buildings around. He thought, "Boy, this is just like being out west." He walked over in front of the next building to read the sign hanging from the front porch. "Clearwater, Missouri," he read.

"This is sure some town Mr. Clark, only two buildings."

"There's one more back up there in the trees," said Mr. Clark, pointing to a small white house several yards back from the road.

Just then Bud's father drove up in front of the store and got out of the car. Bud ran over to him.

"Are we going to buy something here?" he asked.

"No," replied his father. "We must make arrangements to get our mail here."

"How come we won't have a mailbox along the road like all the houses we have passed?" Bud asked. "Because this is the end of the line," his father said with a laugh. "The mail carrier only comes this far and everyone who lives beyond here must pick up their mail here at the post office."

"I don't see any post office," Bud said.

His father laughed again. "It's inside the store. Come on I'll show you." When they stepped into the store it seemed very dark at first because their eyes were used to the bright sunlight. Soon however, Bud could see that one corner of the room was partitioned off and there was one small window with the words Post Office written above it. They stepped up to the window as a small crippled man walked around behind the partition.

"Good morning Mr. Nations." Bud's father said.

"Good Morning" came the reply. "What can I do for you folks today?"

"We are moving into the house on Mr. Clark's farm today and would like to make arrangements to pick up our mail here."

Just then Bud heard the horn on the truck. "I have to go, Pop." He shouted over his shoulder as he ran out the door.

The truck had pulled away from the gas pump and was waiting in front of the store for Bud. He climbed up into the cab and slammed the door. "All set." He said, and away they went. A moment later the truck slowed down and turned to the right off the road. Bud couldn't see anything but water at first, but finally made out the form of a concrete bridge just under the water. It didn't seem big enough for the truck but Mr. Clark didn't hesitate so Bud guessed it must be. Now the road became much smaller. Trees brushed against the truck on both sides and seemed so close that Bud didn't think they could possibly get through in some places. On and on the truck traveled. Suddenly Mr. Clark pointed to a big brick house away up on a hill to their right.

"That's where I live," he said. "You must come over and play with my boys sometime." Bud noticed they had been traveling along a creek for some time and he asked what the name of it was.

"Officially they say it is the North fork of the Little Saline River, but folks around here call it 'Greasy Creek'."

Pretty soon the truck slowed down and they pulled off the road to the left, down the bank and into the creek.

"Well, we're almost there Bud. It's just over the hill up that way."

They pulled up out of the creek and climbed a narrow gravel road over the hill. Up ahead Bud could see an old gray barn with a cement-block silo next to it. He knew from other farm experiences that silos were tall round structures used to store feed for cattle for the wintertime. Then he saw the house, sitting up on the hillside, to the left of the road. As they stopped he could see that this was apparently the end of the road since there was a fence with a closed gate in front of them. Bud could tell that the road beyond the gate was hardly a road at all, but a faint set of ruts that resembled a road.

Chapter 2
Bud's New Home

The house looked very old and much in need of repairs. "There hasn't been much work done on the old place in a long time." Said Mr. Clark. "No one has lived here for several years."

The weeds were very high in the yard and the old wooden shed next to the house seemed about to fall down. What appeared to have been a garage at one time had already fallen down and many of the boards had been carried away. Mr. Clark opened the gate in front of the truck and drove around the yard, up the hill, to the back of the house. The front porch was high off the ground, but the back was at ground level.

"It will be much easier to unload the furniture from up here," said Mr. Clark. "We won't have to carry everything up the steps this way."

Bud wanted to run and investigate everything but his mother and father and sister had arrived and the unloading began. Bud couldn't carry the big heavy pieces but there were many boxes and smaller things for him to take into the house. It seemed to take a long time to unload the big truck but at last everything was moved in and Mr. Clark drove away.

It was late in the evening by this time and Bud was to get his first taste of some of the chores he would have to do in the future. Since there was no electricity here, they could not flip a switch and have the lights come on. Bud's father handed him two glass lamps and told him to take them out in the back yard and fill them with coal oil. When the lamps were full Bud brought them back in the house and his father lit each one with a match. Then he adjusted the wicks to the right height and put the globes on them. They put one of the lamps in the front room and the other in the kitchen.

Bud's father picked up the new white bucket they had bought to get water in.

"Let's go down and see what the spring is like Bud." They walked down to one side of the yard, about twenty feet from the house and came to the spring. All Bud could see was some boards laid side by side on the ground. His father picked up the boards and shined his flashlight under them. There was a hole in the ground about four or five feet square and nearly as deep. The hole was about half full of water. With the light shining into the water they could see a small hole near the bottom on one side. "That's where the water comes out of the ground, isn't it, Pop?"

"Yes Bud, and see the piece of pipe on the other side? That's where the water runs out and into the springhouse over there. You must always remember to dip the bucket into the water very gently when you are filling it. If you get in too big of a hurry and stir up the water it will cause the leaves and dirt on the bottom to mix in with your water and it won't be any good to drink. If this happens you will have to wait for a half hour or more for the water to clear again." Bud's father dipped the bucket into the water gently and let it slowly sink until it was full. Then he lifted the bucket out and they replaced the boards and carried the bucket of fresh water up to the house. The water tasted nice and cold to Bud." It almost seems as if it came from the refrigerator," he said, and they all agreed.

Bud helped his father fix up the big bed that his mother and father slept on. Next they went into another room and fixed the smaller bed for his sister. There was no other room for him and no bed either. He would have to sleep on the couch or daybed as it was called. He had done this many times in the past.

Just before bedtime each one would take the flashlight and go up to the little house on the hill, just beyond, and to one side of the yard. This was commonly known as the outhouse. Bud thought," This will be a long way to come on a cold rainy night." As he walked back to the house he could hear the high-pitched sound of a screech owl somewhere off in the woods. Even though he was familiar with the little bird, the sound was so eerie that he hurried to get inside where he felt more secure. Later, as he snuggled down under the covers for the night, he could still hear the little owl, and from somewhere much farther away came the occasional hooting of an old hoot owl, mixed with the baying of a coon dog hot on the trail. Life was sure going to be different here, he thought, as he drifted off to sleep.

Chapter 3
Life in the Hills

Bud was up with the sun the next morning and began the day by collecting some sticks and limbs to chop up for cook wood for the big range in the kitchen. By the time his mother and sister were up, Bud's father had the stove hot and a kettle of water steaming merrily away. Since there was no hot water heater, all of the water had to be heated on the stove.

After breakfast, while the rest of the family began to unpack and arrange things, Bud was sent to clean out the springhouse. He had never seen a springhouse up close before, but he had heard about one from his parents. First, he had to shovel the dirt and dead leaves away from the door in order to open it. The door squeaked and squawked on its rusty hinges as Bud forced it open.

There was no light inside and no windows to let in the sunshine. Soon his eyes grew accustomed to the dim light. The floor was made of concrete and was covered with debris. Running the length of the building along one side was a concrete trough. Its sides were about a foot above the floor. Cold water from the spring outside flowed through the trough. The hole in the lower end was five or six inches up from the bottom so that the water was always that deep in the trough. Bud cleaned the mud out of the bottom of the trough and swept the springhouse clean. Then he went up to the house and asked his mother what she wanted to put in the springhouse to keep cool. She gave Bud a heavy gallon crock jar nearly full of milk with a plate set on top to keep out the dust. He carefully carried it down to the springhouse and set it gently down into the water. Two more trips were needed to bring the butter and other things, which must be kept cool. He placed several large flat rocks in the trough on which to set plates and small bowls to keep them near the water but not in it.

"This will certainly keep things cool." Bud thought," but it's not nearly as handy as having a refrigerator right in the kitchen."

He would soon find there was another problem with springhouses. Not only did they keep food items cool, but in hot weather snakes enjoyed the coolness as well. Lizards, crawdads and even possums sometimes cooled off in the outdoor refrigerator. Everything had to be well covered and Bud had to watch out for wildlife each time he made a trip for his mother.

That afternoon Mr. Clark drove up to the house in his big truck. He backed off the road against a bank and led a red and black brindle cow out of the truck. As he was doing this, Bud and his father walked down to talk to him.

"Hello there," Said Mr. Clark. "I've brought you a cow to milk, Bud. She needs to be milked and we have more milk than we know what to do with at home, so I thought you could use her. Besides I figured you needed something to keep you busy." He said, with a wink to Bud's father. His father laughed and placed a hand on Bud's shoulder.

"I don't think he'll have much trouble finding something to do, but one more chore shouldn't do any harm."

"Where'll we keep the cow?" asked Bud.

"Well," said Mr. Clark," there's no fenced in pasture here, so I guess she'll go just about where she pleases. We do have a fence around part of the place so the only way she can go is back in the hills behind the house there."

"Well, what if she just keeps on going and don't come back?" Bud asked.

"I don't think you'll have to worry about that Bud. We have some more cows out there and we keep some salt for them near the barn here so they keep coming back. Besides, the only good drinking water they have most of the time is in the creek below the spring here, so they won't get too far from that."

Little did Bud realize then the number of hours he would spend hunting for Bossy, as they named her. And even more time consuming was the frustrating task of trying to bring her back to the house for a milking twice a day. She never wanted to leave the other cows and they were never in a mood to come to the house when it was milking time. Bud always managed to win out in the end, but he sure lost his patience many times. Sometimes he would end up running several miles altogether by the time he got Bossy to the house. Bud didn't have big strong hands like his father yet, but milking the cow helped to strengthen them and it wasn't long before he was doing a pretty good job of milking.

One of Bud's biggest jobs was getting in the firewood. It seemed as if the wood box behind the cook stove was always empty. In the past, many trees had been cut for lumber in the hills around the house. Later, Mr. Clark had sawn up many of the limbs for firewood. There were still little piles of wood that had not been used, scattered around in the woods. Bud's job was to find these and carry the wood back to the house. The smaller pieces were used for cook wood and the larger ones were stacked away on the back porch for use in the heating stove when winter came.

After they were pretty well settled in their new home Bud and his father went out to an old shed near the house. The shed had fallen down but much of the lumber was still useable. They got enough boards to build a small chicken house up on the hillside behind the house. Some of their friends gave them a few chickens to get started with and so Bud's list of chores became a little longer. The chickens had to be fed every day, the eggs had to be gathered, and every few weeks the area under the roost had to be cleaned out.

Then, there was the garden to be taken care of. The ground around their house was so rocky it would not be very good for a garden. Mr. Clark had suggested that they plant a garden with him. It was about a mile or so from where Bud lived to where the shared garden would be. His father decided to combine both ideas. They would make a small garden next to their yard to try to raise a few things, and join with Mr. Clark and do the rest of their gardening at his house. This, of course, meant many walks down the creek road to either work on the garden or gather food from it. At times Bud would have a chance to play with the Clark boys. One of their favorite things to do was to find some large overripe cucumbers, carve them into boats and float them down the creek, trying to sink them by throwing rocks at them.

As we just saw all was not work along the creek. Some days his friend Jimmy Boyd would ride down on one of his father's horses, and together they would ride around in the hills along "Greasy Creek." One day as they rode up over a steep hogback, there stood one of the biggest bucks Bud had ever seen. He had just come up over the other side and they met face-to-face right at the top. The deer was so startled he just stood there and looked at them for a long moment. Then he turned around and bounded stiff-legged, back the way he had come with Bud and Jimmy hot on his trail. Of course a horse is no match for a deer anytime and with two riders on this one the race was over before it really got started. Bud had often jumped deer up in the old apple orchard when he went early in the morning to find Bossy, but they never ceased to thrill him as they bounded off down the hillside in their ground shaking, stiff-legged fashion.

Bud's grandfather came down from St. Louis every few weeks and he would take Bud in his big dump truck to other fishing spots that were too far away for him to walk to. His grandmother used to kid them about living so far back in the hills that the sunshine had to be piped in to them.

Bud always looked forward to seeing his grandparents. He had so much fun fishing and hunting with his grandpa. Bud's father was so busy trying to make a living for them that he had little time to spend with Bud. He rarely went fishing or hunting with them. They would usually take their dinner and spend the whole day and part of the night on the creek or riverbank. Many times they came home empty handed, but they still had a lot of fun. Bud was always happy to see his grandma too, for that meant biscuits for breakfast. Bud's mother was a very good cook, but she didn't like to bake biscuits. Every time his grandma came she would bake a big batch of biscuits for breakfast, each morning. Bud thought there was nothing better than hot biscuits, butter, gravy, eggs and a big glass of cold milk to top it off. As Bud's father would say grace before the meal and thank God for their many blessings, Bud would see in his mind a piece of paper listing the blessings and, a big plate of biscuits would be number one. Then he would think," How lucky I am to have such wonderful grandparents."

Bud also spent time alone along the creek. At times he would fish for the hog-suckers and sunfish that could be found in the deeper water holes along the usually shallow creek. At other times he would skip small flat rocks across the creek, or throw rocks at floating sticks, or maybe practice with the slingshot his grandfather had made for him from an old inner-tube and a forked branch from a tree limb. He could always find something to occupy his time when he wasn't doing chores.

On Greasy Creek, ,as on most country streams, everyone had at least one dog, and often more than one. Since raccoons, which are usually shortened to coons, are found along any stream, most country homes included one or more coon hounds among their pets. Coon hunting was common with the men along the ozark streams since it gave them a chance to get together and swap yarns, usually relating to other hunts or special dogs. Many of the hunters were very partial to certain breeds and often were quiet ready to argue on their behalf, as they lay or sit around a small fire and listened for the dogs to pick up a coons trail. Each one knew the sound of his dogs and could tell if they were on a hot or cold track and if they treed the coon or not. Since coon meat was considered as good eating, the hunts were justified if food was brought home.

Hunting and fishing had always helped to supplement the supply of meat in Bud's home, but he did not have a dog of his own when they moved to their new home. However, his grand mother soon took care of that. One day while sitting on her front steps, in St. Louis, she saw a boy coming towards her carrying a little white puppy. She just had to see the cute little dog and pet it. As she talked to the boy she learned he was taking the puppy to one of his friends, but there was one more at home that he needed to give away. She had him bring the remaining puppy to her, and on their next trip to Greasy Creek Bud got a very pleasant surprise. It wasn't a hound dog, but rather a mixture of breeds often called a heins dog, due to the advertising by the Heins Ketchup Company that they had 57 varieties.

The puppy had already been named Bouncer, because of his lively antics while playing. Bouncer grew rapidly, and soon was running after Bud wherever he went. As for hunting Bouncer had some good points and some bad ones. He was good to get into places Bud couldn't, but he ran around so much he often scared up the rabbits or quails before Bud or his grandpa could get close enough to shoot them.

Bud and his father had planted some beans in a nearby cornfield so the beans could climb up the cornstalks. One day Bud and Bouncer went to check on the beans, to see if they were ready for picking. Bud noticed that Bouncer was acting strangely, for him. Usually he was on the run, trying to check everywhere and still keep ahead of Bud. But this time he was standing very still, and staring intently at something a short distance beyond where he stood. Bud stopped to watch what the dog would do. Just then Bouncer darted forward and grabbed a rabbit which he tossed in the air. In fact he threw the rabbit over his back, where it landed on it's feet and was gone in a flash, with Bouncer hot on his trail. Needless to say, the rabbit won the race, but a happy little dog was soon coming back with his tongue hanging out and his sides heaving. He almost seemed to be saying, I sure scared that rabbit half to death.

On another occasion Bud and Bouncer would meet up with a big groundhog. Caught away from his hole, the groundhog backed into a hollow tree just big enough to hold him. For sometime Bouncer and the hog discussed the situation, each daring the other to make the first move. It seemed to Bud that the more they talked the louder they got and the closer they came to each other. Finally things came to a quick end. Bouncer got a little too close and the groundhog bit his nose. That was more than Bouncer could take, so he waded in, grabbed the groundhog by the neck, and dragged him out of the tree, shaking him back and forth. Bouncer turned loose for a moment and Bud grabbed him by the collar, pulling him away, and giving the groundhog a chance to waddle back to his hole.

Once again Bouncer seemed to be very pleased with his conquest and ready to look for another. For years to come Bud and Bouncer would be nearly inseparable, but their time on Greasy Creek would never be forgotten. Eventually they had to move to a place in town where they could not keep a dog. They found a family that would adopt Bouncer, so he went to a good home.

Bud would always regret the fact that he never got to go on a coon hunt. He could remember his father telling about a hunt he and his brothers had been on when still young boys. Two of his brothers made plans to scare others in the group. They lived so far from the nearest town that most of them had never seen a game warden. So most of the farmers, who hunted on their own farms, never bothered to buy a hunting permit. They just never expected to get caught. The men and boys were all sitting around a small fire swapping yarns when the two brothers put their plan into action. One of his brothers excused himself to answer a call from mother nature and walked off into the darkness. They knew that all of the group would be staring into the fire most of the time, and so could not see very well when suddenly looking into the darkness around them. The one that had excused himself quietly slipped around to the other side of the group where there was a fence. He pretended to be climbing the fence, which of course made a noise. The brother still by the fire yelled, "game warden," and jumped up and ran into the darkness. Since none of the men bothered to buy hunting permits they all followed his action, and soon all had headed for their homes. The supposed game warden kicked out the fire and went home as well, laughing all the way. The others eventually found out what had happened, and at first were not very happy about it. However, they soon got over it and began to laugh and make jokes about the way they had been fooled.

Although Bud never was able to go on a coon hunt, he did get to eat their meat on several occasions. He found it to be very good, as he did most wild meat.

Speaking of meat, did you ever wonder where the sausage or ham that you enjoy so much, came from, other than the store. Many farmers, or just people who live in the country, butcher their own meat. Bud was surprised one Sunday after church, when Mr. Patterson ask if he and his parents would like to help butcher several hogs. Since his father had worked as a butcher in St. Louis, for nearly eight years, this was nothing new to him. But Bud had never been involved in the process before, and looked forward to it. On Monday morning they went to Patterson's farm. People had been getting things ready for some time, and were ready to start when they arrived. Bud went with Billy to watch him shoot the first hog. Bang! With one shot from his 22 caliber rifle, the hog dropped in his tracks. Billy tied a piece of strong rope to one of the hogs hind legs, as other men came to help drag it to the butchering spot. There was a big oak tree at the spot, which had a large limb about a dozen feet off the ground. There was a long rope wrapped around several pulleys, called a block and tackle, used to hoist the hog in the air so it could be worked on easier. To do this a slit was cut in each back leg, just above the hoof.. A strong stick had been cut from a hickory tree and sharpened at both ends. This was worked through the slits in the hogs legs, then tied in the middle to the block and tackle. The men then lifted the hog and pulled it over to a barrel filled with very hot water. It was let down into the water, then pulled out and scraped with a knife to get the hair off. The hogs skin is then. split from tail to neck, down the stomach, and the insides taken out. Most people thought the next job was the worst in the butchering process. Someone had to take the large intestine and clean it out, turn the inside out and scrub it with soap and brush to get it completely clean. Then it was hung out to dry, so it could later be stuffed with sausage. While this was being done, some were keeping the fire going under the barrel of hot water. They also kept the barrel full of water. Others were cutting up the meat into hams, chops, bacon, ground meat for sausage and other lesser items. Some were busy cooking dinner for all of the workers. Some were busy with the smoke house, getting the fires going, keeping them burning and cutting and sharpening hickory sticks to hang the meat up for smoking. Still others were busy rubbing salt or sugar into and onto some of the meat to keep it from spoiling. It was a long, very busy day for everyone but when it ended there was enough pork put away to last them for a year. Also no neighbor went home empty handed. Some Patterson pork found its way to each home that sent someone to help. Bud's families share was to include two cured hams, to be given to heart surgeons at Missouri Baptist Hospital in St. Louis. His mother had to have a heart operation a few months before, and the two doctors who performed the surgery, knowing they had little money, asked for a ham apiece, if his church members could provide them when they did their butchering. It is messy work with nothing pleasant about it, yet everyone felt good about a job well done, and working together with friends. Everyone would sleep good that night, even Patterson's dogs and cats were well fed and content.

As with any group of people anywhere, not everyone in this area lived or did everything in the same way. Bud thought about some of the differences and guessed it must reflect the fact that they came from different countries where things were done in different ways. He felt this must be a good thing, since each one could learn new things from their neighbors, if they wanted to.

Chapter 4
Church in a Log Cabin

Bud's father was a preacher. He always tried to live as near as possible to the church where he preached. This was why they had moved to Greasy Creek. It was sometimes hard to find a house where they could live near the church. At this time his father was a half-time preacher at two different churches. This meant that he would preach in one church two Sundays a month and in the other church, two Sundays a month. Bud always looked forward to the months that had five Sundays in them. Each time this happened, several of the churches in the area would get together for what they called a fifth-Sunday meeting. There would be tables full of the most delicious food and deserts. Each family would bring more than enough to feed their own family.

One lady, who knew what Bud liked, would always bring a big bowl of the best dumplings Bud had ever eaten. There was only one thing wrong with these meals; there just wasn't enough room in his stomach for all he wanted to eat. There would be preaching and singing after the meal.

The preaching was fine with Bud as he was often too full to run and play with the other kids. It felt good just to sit still and wait for the food to digest. He wasn't too sure about the singing though. He wondered if he opened his mouth too wide, if something besides his voice might come out.

One of the churches where Bud's father preached was a log cabin. It was named the "Pine Log Church" because it was built of pine logs. There was nothing fancy about the little church, either inside or out. In fact, except for the cross hanging over the door, you would not even know it was a church.

There were no stained glass windows, no rugs on the floor, and no fancy decorations or pictures. The men had made the hard wooden benches from pine lumber. In the middle of the floor, near the front, stood an old potbellied stove. The pipe for the smoke stood straight up several feet, then, bent over and led to the rock chimney at the back of the church.

Across the end of the church, a low platform had been built. This held a homemade speaker stand and some wooden chairs for the choir. To one side of the church just below the platform, stood an upright piano, much in need of tuning. There were no classrooms for the Sunday School to meet in. They had fastened wires to the walls and strung them across the church so that curtains could be hung on them, to divide the room into several smaller classrooms. When the classes were over, the curtains were pushed back against the walls, out of the way. For nighttime meetings, there was a row of lamps along each side of the church, fastened to the walls. It was hard to read the songbooks with such dim light.

On warm days the windows would be opened to let in fresh air. Bud usually sat next to a window so he could see whatever went on outside. There were always birds flying around and occasionally a couple of wayward squirrels that had skipped church and were playing tag in one of the trees outside the window.

On one particular Sunday morning, it was rather cool and the windows were closed. Bud was sitting next to one, as usual. His friend Bob was sitting next to him and they were both very interested in a fly that was buzzing angrily while attempting to find a way out through the windowpane. Bob leaned over and whispered in Bud's ear, "Catch him for me." Bud made several carefully timed attempts before catching it in his hand. It wasn't easy to catch a moving fly while trying to keep one eye on his father, to avoid any future trouble. Bud was sure his father would not realize the importance of fulfilling such a request, during one of his sermons. With the fly at last in his fist, Bud reached in carefully and picked it up between his fore finger and thumb and handed it to Bob. Whack! Bob smashed the fly all over Bud's fingers with a well-aimed blow of his rolled up Sunday School book. Bud was so surprised he just sat without moving, for a long moment. This was all that saved him from a good licking when he got home. His father, and everyone else looked over to see what the noise was all about. All they saw was Bob sitting there trying unsuccessfully to restrain his laughter and Bud sitting next to him doing nothing. Bud managed to retain his solemn expression long enough to avoid being seen, but the more he thought about what had happened, the funnier it seemed to get. He bent over to tie his shoes in order to let out a low snicker or two that just couldn't wait. Of course Bud had to explain to his father, after church, that Bob had just swatted a fly that was pestering them and that he hadn't thought it would make so much noise.

At times Bud felt a little guilty for not paying more attention to what was being said in church. But somehow, he couldn't seem to keep his mind from wandering. If it was light outside, he could watch the squirrels playing tag in the trees around the church. Birds flew back and forth busily engaged in finding food. There were usually one or two hounds that were very religious and came to church each Sunday. They even attended the services when they could sneak in the door. However, most of the time they were nosing around trying to scare up a rabbit or anything else they could chase for a while to liven up the day.

At night there was nothing to see outside so Bud had to settle for what he could picture in his imagination. Since he had a very active imagination he managed to accomplish an awful lot during the period of a sermon. One night, thanks to Bob, his daydreaming led to trouble. Bud was sitting with one leg across the other. In his mind he was somewhere off in the wilderness exploring unknown lands. The idea suddenly came to Bob that Bud's leg was in just the right position for a test of his reflexes. There was nothing wrong with Bud's reflexes and his leg responded exactly as Bob had hoped it would. WHAM! Bud's foot hit the seat in front of him with a resounding crash. Naturally, everyone in church looked around to see what the noise was all about. Bud felt like crawling under his seat, but it was too late to do anything but sit there and look guilty. After this little episode, his father decided things would run more smoothly during the church services if Bud would sit with his mother instead of Bob.

Since my dad had to hold a working position besides his preaching, our Sunday afternoons were usually spent visiting people who lived in the community where he was preaching. Sometimes these visits led to very interesting side effects. This is one of those occasions. We were on our way to visit a family that lived a good way off the main road. Since this was a farm the land was fenced with a gate at the entrance. Dad had closed the gate after we entered and had driven only a short way when he stopped the car and got out. It seemed that Mother Nature was calling and dad had found a private place behind some trees where the call could be answered. Being in a bit of a hurry he left the keys in the car. My mom, who had never driven a car, felt this would be a good time to learn. The only problem was that she had no teacher.

However, mom thought she had seen dad go through the operation so many times she could do the same.

As usual she was right, up to one very critical step. She got the car started, put into gear and stepped on the gas. Away we went but the road kept shifting about so fast mom could not keep the car on it. Bushes and trees were also moving around and kept getting in our way. Some of the bushes came off second best but fortunately the trees managed to get out of the way up to this point. Suddenly, dad appeared on the running board of the old Model A Ford and he kept telling mom to step on the brake, which she did. However, she still had the other foot on the gas so we kept going. Dad then said step on the clutch which mom did by taking her foot off the brake. Of course the car kept moving and the engine revved up to a high speed. Dad knew if she took her foot off the clutch the sudden force of the fast moving engine just might tear up the transmission so rather than give any more instructions to mom he reached in and turned the key off. With the key off the engine and the car gradually came to a stop, as did moms first and only driving lesson. As was often said in those days, "all's well that ends well."

Chapter 5

Church in A Town that Used to Be

Every other Sunday Bud's father preached at another church several miles away. This church was in the little town of Coffman. Bud liked to call it the town that used to be because most of it was gone now. Coffman had been a thriving little community in its 'heyday." However, that time was long past. Bud liked to explore the old buildings with his friends whenever he got a chance. Usually someone in the church would invite them home for Sunday dinner. When it happened to be in the home of one of his friends who lived in town, they could sometimes spend the afternoon wandering through the remains.

Approximately a dozen families, some of whom were related, were still living in Coffman. An old railroad track bed ran along the lower side of town.

The tracks had been taken up and even the ties had been dug up and hauled off by the farmers in the area. One of the older men in the church had told him that the tracks had belonged to a company called the Blackhawk Railroad. At one time there had even been a train station in Coffman. All that remained was a pile of rotten boards grown over with weeds. Near the spot where the train station stood, there had been a one-operator telephone office.

Evidently this building had been torn down and the lumber hauled away, for Bud couldn't find any evidence of it. The gravel road formed a rectangle around the town, which was located on a hillside. On one of the lower corners near the old track bed stood a large false fronted building. It was rather spooky looking to Bud. No one had used the building for many years and it was in a rather dilapidated condition. This had at one time been one of the town's two general stores. The other was still in operation up on the hill on the opposite corner of town. The door on the old store building was kept locked so Bud was never able to see what the inside looked like.

There was another smaller building next to the store, which housed the local beer joint. Up on the hill in back of the store stood what remained of an old log cabin. This upper corner of the town was uninhabited. The part of the town still in use lay on the other end of the rectangle with the homes being mostly on the lower part. On the upper end, across from the store that was still in operation, stood a neat freshly painted white church house. It even had stained glass windows and a well-kept graveyard in back. Next to it stood a white house where the priest lived. This was the only Catholic Church for many miles around, so people came from all over to attend mass here.

Going down the road the other way from the store was an old weather worn, one room church house and schoolhouse standing next to each other. A religious group known as the Camelites had abandoned the church house many years before. The building had been white at one time but was now just a weather-beaten grey. It leaned to one side as if it were tired and was in the act of lying down. This is where Bud would attend church for the next several years. A lot of work had to be done before the building was useable. The building had to be straightened and reinforced. The inside covered with wall boarding and painted. At first they used coal-oil lamps for lighting. Later a gas lantern was used, and finally, electric lights were installed. There was an ancient pump organ covered with dust in one corner of the building. This was cleaned up and repaired enough to be useable for some time until a piano could be obtained.

Three big soft chairs in the front of the church were very badly worn and had to be taken away to an upholstery shop to be recovered. The churchyard was one big mud hole each time it rained and had to be graveled before it was useable. All of the people pitched in and worked hard and soon had a pretty little white church house, complete with steeple and bell, ready for services. The parking lot was quite a sight the first Sunday in the new church. There were cars of various vintage including a 29 Model A Ford and 28 Chevrolet, farm trucks both large and small, a horse drawn wagon, one saddle horse, and two bicycles. Of course there was also the usual collection of faithful hounds, unwilling to miss any kind of meeting where they might renew old acquaintances and make some new ones. Due to the faithfulness of the dogs, the local cats rarely had a chance to attend church.

Sometimes after church they would stop at the general store to get gas. Bud had never seen a gas pump like these before coming to Coffman. They had a tall glass tank on top of the pump marked and numbered for each gallon it could hold. The storeowner would push and pull on a big lever on the side of the pump and the red gasoline would rise higher and higher in the glass tank. When the gas reached the number of gallons in the tank that the customer wished to buy he would quite pumping. Then he would place the hose into the cars gas tank and drain the gas in the pump to the car. No electricity was involved in this process, just arm strength and gravity, but it worked just fine. Sometimes Bud and his sister were allowed to buy a soda or some ice cream, but that was rare because his father did not make much money.

Chapter 6

Flash Flood

Greasy Creek was usually a quiet, easy-going stream. It was not more than six to ten inches deep in the area where Bud lived. They could tell that it sometimes got much higher when it flooded but they had never seen it get very much deeper. One Sunday morning while they were in church in Coffman it began to rain. For a while it really poured down but no one thought much about it. Hard rains were not uncommon in Missouri and the farmers needed the water for their crops. On their way home after church, Buds dad stopped at the store in Clearwater to pick up a loaf of bread. His mother had been ill that day and his grandparents were at home with her.

Mr. Nations told Bud's father that he probably wouldn't be able to get home for some time because the creek was up too high. He said one of the people living near the creek had been in the store a short time before and said that it looked like a wall of water ten feet high coming down the creek while they were watching. Since they had never seen it get too deep in the past they did not expect it to be too much of a problem. Besides, they had a sick mother plus their grandparents waiting for them at home so they would have to give it a try. They didn't have far to go to get to where they could see some of the affects of the flood. Just a short distance down the hill below the store they had to turn off on a smaller side-road and cross a small creek that had a low-water concrete bridge somewhere under the water. As they crept slowly into the flood the water rose higher and higher on the front of the car. Soon the headlights were submerged, Bud's father decided it would be best to back out and wait for the water to go down a bit.

After waiting about an hour the water seemed to recede a bit so they decided to give it another try. This time they made it through but their relief only lasted a few minutes when they found the road along the creek was now a part of the creek and was soon impassable again. Another hours wait seemed much longer but at last they were able to make it all the way to where they had to cross the creek to get to their home. Here another wait was in order. It turned out to be much longer and they began to feel the affects of missing lunch.

After waiting two more hours they could tell the water level was dropping a bit. They could see some small rocks beginning to show up several feet out from the edge of the water. Bud's dad decided it was time to try driving across, the car moved slowly forward and they could tell it was not on firm footing. The bed of the stream was usually solid rock although a bit rough. However, they seemed to be on loose rock or gravel which surprised his father. All at once the front end of the car plunged much lower in the water and the engine stopped running.

Water was flowing through the floor of the car and they were all standing in their seats. The car bouncing down stream and Bud looked out at the water, which was just about to come in the window on his side of the car. His father quickly removed his right shoe and stuck his foot into the water in the floor of the car. Bud could hear the sound of the starter motor turning the engine over as if trying to start. Of course the engine couldn't start but ever so slowly it began to back out of the deeper, swifter flowing water. This could not take them very far but reduced the danger a good bit. They were very fortunate that the car had not rolled over from the force of the current and it now looked like there would be another long wait since the water was going down very slowly and they were no longer near the bank where they might have been able to wade out.

Fortunately their neighbor, Mr. Boyd, who lived farther up the creek drove by in his pickup truck and saw their car in the creek. He had to cross the creek several times to get to his home but he was used to doing this and knew a trick to help him avoid the problems Buds family had just gone through. He kept a lot of weight in the bed of his truck and he took the fan belt off so the fan would not throw water back on the engine, which would drown it out and leave him stalled in the water. He told us not to go anywhere with a laugh and said he would be back shortly with some rope to pull them out.

Sure enough, he soon returned with a long rope on a wagon pulled by a team of horses. In the meantime Bud's grandpa had driven his dump truck down to the other side of the creek. Mr. Boyd got down in the water and tied the rope to our car. Then he drove his team and wagon across the creek and tied the other end of the rope to grandpa's truck. When he was done grandpa pulled us across the creek which was still very high and swift and made for a scary ride which took us farther down the stream as we were being pulled across. After we had been pulled up to our house Mr. Boyd took his rope and headed home. After a brief, late, dinner Bud's grandparents needed to head for home. Buds father was going with them as far as Clearwater so he could buy oil and other fluids that would have to be changed in their car.

Bud followed them back down to the creek and watched as his grandfather drove into the water too fast and drowned out his engine. His dad crawled out on the trucks fender and raised the hood over the motor so he could use a towel to dry off the parts of the engine that had water splashed on them. Soon they had the truck running and were on their way. Bud was to spend a long wait and it began to get darker when his father finally appeared on the other bank of the still flooded creek. Bud was very worried about his father trying to cross the creek with a heavy load of cans. His father took off his pants and tied each leg in a knot. He then put the cans of oil into the pant legs and set them on his shoulder as he waded into the bone chilling cold floodwater. The waters rose up and up until they were well above his waist as he leaned into the swift current.

Bud could barely see him as he slowly felt his way across and prayed there would not be any trees or logs come down the stream and hit his father. At last he made it across and put his pants and shoes back on. He handed some of the cans to Bud and they made their way up to the house. Since his dad would have to go to work in the morning very early they had to change out all the fluids in the car that night. Bud held the flashlight so his dad could see how to do the work.

By the next morning Greasy Creek was almost back to normal. Bud and his dad walked down to the creek to check it out and be sure the car could make it across to go to work. They could now see what had happened to them the day before. Not only had a large bank of gravel and small rocks been washed into the place where they had driven into the water but there was also a small rut cut into the bank at a right angle. This was what had stopped them from being washed on down the creek.

As Bud thought about the experience he hoped he would never get into another flood. There were other smaller floods after that but they never got into one again. They had learned very well what Greasy Creek could do and had a greater respect for its strength. The next time this happened they tried to drive out over the hills behind the house. However the rain had turned the hillside to mud and they could not make it out. After that when it began to rain at night Bud's dad would park the car at the top of the hill so they could make it out to another road and take a long way around to wherever they needed to go.

Chapter 7
An Old-Fashioned Farm

Some of the families where Bud went to church
had no cars but only traveled by horseback or in a
buckboard, which is a wagon with a spring-mounted
seat in front. One of the families invited Bud to stay
with them for a few days to help put up hay. Bud
was so excited he could hardly wait for the hay to
grow high enough to cut. At last the day arrived and
Bud got to ride home in the buckboard. He even
got to drive the team of horses part of the way. He
was going to stay with Mr. and Mrs. Griffith for a
whole week. It seemed to take a long time to get to
their house in the buckboard. They had to cross a
creek near the house so they stopped in the creek
for a while to let the horses rest, cool off, and get
a drink. When the horses had drank their fill, they
moved on, climbing up and around a small hill on

the other side of the creek. As they rounded the hill the Griffith's home came into view. They lived in a small, hand hewn, log cabin. There was a log barn and some other log buildings used for storage and a hen house and sheep shed.

It looked like some storybook picture of a western ranch, complete with horses in the corral. There was even a cowboy riding down the wagon trail to meet them. They pulled to a stop as the man on the horse approached them. Bud could see that it was Grandpa Griffith, who lived farther up in the hills and always traveled by horseback. After a brief talk, Mr. Griffith shook the reins and the horses moved on towards the house.

The wagon stopped near the front door of the cabin and Bud got his first lesson in how to unhook a team of horses. After the horses were unhooked and put in the barnyard, Bud and Mr. Griffith walked up to the cabin. Bud was suddenly reminded that it was past his usual lunchtime as they were greeted with the smell of fried ham coming from the kitchen. After a quick wash-up in the pan of cold water, and tossing it out the back door, they were all set for lunch. A big meal of fried ham, mashed potatoes, roasting' ears, sliced tomatoes, home made bread and, milk, had Bud ready for some exploring. Knowing what boys always liked to do, Mr. Griffith suggested that Bud go for a ride on one of the horses. Whooping with joy Bud tore out of the house, nearly knocking the screen-door off its hinges. The yard gate slammed behind him with a bang almost before the screen door had slammed shut. By the time Mr. Griffith had reached the barn, Bud had picked out a pretty little dun colored mustang and led her up to the harness room. There Mr. Griffith explained all about how to saddle the horse properly. Bud was soon on his way down the road. After going a short distance down the road he turned off onto a path that he had seen Grandpa Griffith ride. He knew that the old man lived by himself somewhere back up in the hills and he wanted to see where it was.

As they splashed across a small stream Bud stopped the cowpony for a drink of the cool, clear water. Out of sight of the house now and all alone, Bud could really imagine himself to be a mountain man, exploring the wilderness where no white man had been before. Leaving the stream behind, they climbed a wooded ridge with oak, walnut, and hickory trees. At last they entered a clearing from which they could see far off along the hillsides and the valley below. Bud stopped the horse once again to let it rest and to enjoy the beautiful scenery.

As he sat there quietly a movement in the distance caught his eye. Several hundred yards away a deer stepped daintily across another small clearing and in a moment was followed by a second then a third and fourth and finally well behind the others, a large buck stepped cautiously into the clearing and then crossed quickly and disappeared into the forest. Not a sound had come to Bud's ears and the whole scene seemed almost like a dream. Bud spoke to the horse and they moved quickly along the trail climbing higher and higher into the hills. At last they entered another clearing containing an old weathered log cabin. Bud assumed this small two-roomed place was Grandpa Griffith's home. There was a shed out back that showed signs of a horse being kept there and a small pile of hay lay in the open loft. Somehow the place seemed very lonesome to Bud and even a bit spooky since he was by himself, so he decided it was time to head for home. Upon reaching the cabin Bud unsaddled the horse and turned it loose in the corral. Then he went in the house to tell Mr. and Mrs. Griffith all about his ride.

Early next morning Mr. Griffith woke Bud up and asked how his shooting' eye was doing. Sensing a chance to go hunting, Bud assured him it was in fine shape. Mr. Griffith handed him an old single shot 22 rifle and a box of shells and told him to head up on the hill and see if he could get some fresh squirrel meat for breakfast. Bud lost no time in heading for the woods and was soon seated on a stump in the area of several large hickory trees. It wasn't long before the stillness was broken by the thump of a hickory nut falling to the ground a short distance away. Bud had learned from his grandpa that this was a good indication of squirrels feeding. Very cautiously he tiptoed along in the direction the sound came from. Stopping from time to time to listen he soon heard a faint chipping sound as a squirrel gnawed his way through the tough outer hull of a green hickory nut. Straining his eyes and moving about slowly he soon picked out a large red-coated Fox squirrel sitting high up in the branches eating his breakfast. Taking careful aim, Bud knocked him from the limb with the first shot. No sooner had the sound rang out than a scurrying sound among the branches told Bud there was another squirrel feeding in the same tree. It took only a few minutes for him to slip around and spot the second one watching around the side of the trunk and a moment later Bud was headed for home swinging two nice fat fox squirrels by the tails. Every morning that week breakfast consisted of fried squirrel, fried apples, biscuits and gravy. What more could a guy ask for?!

A shout was heard from somewhere outside the house and Mr. Griffith said, 'the Patterson boys must be here. They were to come over and help me put up some hay as soon as they finished their chores at home." Bud knew the boys well and was glad to have them there. Both Billy and Alvie were huge young men with tremendous strength. Bud had once seen them take turns lifting the front end of their '28 Chevy right off the ground. By the time breakfast was over the Patterson boys had the team of horses hitched to the hay frame so they all headed for the field. There Bud saw neat shocks of hay already stacked and waiting to be hauled away. As they approached the first shocks of hay Alvie and Billy each grabbed a pitchfork and jumped off opposite sides of the wagon. The younger of the two boys, Billy, lifted over half of the first shock in one fork-full and threw it on the wagon. Alvie laughed. "You'll be all day getting a load at that rate."

Then placing his fork near the bottom of a shock he lifted the entire mass of hay onto the wagon.

"Hold on boys," said Mr. Griffith. "Have pity on the poor pitchforks. No wonder your dad can't keep handles in his forks. You guys don't know when to quit. The next thing you know you'll have Bud covered up." Soon they were headed for the barn bouncing merrily along on a big load of hay. When they reached the barn they stopped under the overhanging "dog house" on the end of the barn and unhooked the team. They took the team to the other end of the barn and hooked them up to a large rope lying on the ground. The rope ran through a pulley attached to the barn near the ground, up the side of the barn, through another pulley hanging from the roof, then along the track and was attached to a big hay-fork which Mr. Griffith pulled down with a smaller rope and forced it into the pile of hay on the wagon. He would then holler to the boys on the other end of the barn and they would slap the horses a bit and make them pull the huge fork full of hay up into the barn. When it reached the right point in the barn Mr. Griffith jerked on the small rope and tripped the fork, causing all the hay to drop onto the floor of the hayloft. Then the horses were brought back to where they had started and the fork was pulled back down to pick up another load.

Sometimes Mr. Griffith would take another team of horses to the field and mow down some more hay. Bud would follow the mower around the field while the other boys raked and stacked the hay for hauling to the barn. Sometimes the mower would scare up some young rabbits and Bud would chase one until he caught it. It was fun to pet the soft little bunnies. He wished he could keep them but he knew they would be so scared they would not eat and so would die if they were not turned loose.

One day while the Patterson boys were not there to help, Mr. Griffith had Bud drive the team as they pulled the hay up into the barn. One time, the fork picked up such a big load of hay that it would not fit in the overhanging doghouse at the top of the barn. Mr. Griffith thought that the horses were just not pulling very hard. He shouted to Bud to slap them with the end of the reins to make them pull harder. When Bud did this the horses lunged hard against the load and the doubletree broke with a snap. This is the piece of very strong wood that fastens between the horses and the load for them to pull on. While they were pulling the load the doubletree would raise off the ground to a height of nearly four feet. Bud was standing right behind this whenever it broke and one end of it caught him right across the chest, knocking him about twenty feet away. The blow knocked the wind out of Bud and he lay on the ground trying to get his breathing back.

Mr. Griffith and Mrs. Griffith both had heard the doubletree snap and also heard it hit Bud. They both came running to see just what had happened. They became very worried when they saw him on the ground struggling to breath. They didn't really know what was wrong or what to do for him. However, Bud had this same type of thing happen to him before and seemed to realize that his breathing would return right away. He tried to let them know he would be alright but there was no way he could say anything. Luckily he got his breath back right away and was able to reassure them that he wasn't really hurt bad, just a little sore.

All too soon for Bud, the fields were cleaned and the barn was full of hay for the winter. It was time to go back home again. It had been such a wonderful week Bud knew he would always remember the good times he had on Mr. Griffith's farm.

Chapter 8
School Days

The summer passed swiftly for Bud. Greasy Creek was down to little more than a trickle except for a few of the deeper holes of water which held out bravely against the hot August sun. There was a chill in the night air now and a few of the leaves were starting to put on their fall colors. The dew on the morning grass was much heavier and Bud's pant legs and shoes were soaked by the time he brought old Bossy in for her morning milking. Bud had to get up earlier these days to get his chores completed in time for school. Bud's sister rode with their father as he went to work. He would drop her off at the store in Clearwater where she would catch the school bus for a 40-mile ride into Ste. Genevieve to the high school. Bud hated school buses and was very thankful not to have to go along.

It was 2 or 3 miles through the woods to the Pine Log School where he would be attending. Most of the kids walked to school from the surrounding farms. One of the boys who had been raised in the area had agreed to show Bud the way through the woods and after a couple of errors which made him late for school, he had the way well memorized. He started out along Greasy Creek where the Papaws were beginning to turn purple and would soon be ripe, over the hill to the right.

The trail passed through a large patch of persimmon trees. Look out for the little orange pumpkins. If they were too firm, they would sure pucker ones mouth. Deeper into the woods, watch for the deer which often slept along the trail and were very much of a surprise if one were daydreaming. Past the spooky old farm buildings abandoned to the wind and brush many years before. Over another hill or two and down into Possum Hollow. Here Bud always yelled and whistled, then stood quietly and listened to the echoes bounce back and forth and gradually die away. Often there would come an answering shout and Bud would race down into the valley to meet Jimmy and his sisters and their cousin on their way to school too. Next it was over the open fields to the gray, weather-beaten home of the Hawthorns. If they were not already gone, there would be four more to join in for the walk up the last hill, through the long cornfield and at last reach the little white schoolhouse.

Each day usually began with Bud and the other older boys building a fire in the coal furnace in the basement while the rest of the kids stood over the single large outlet in the floor and try to warm up before going to their seats. The teacher, who had to act as custodian and principal as well as teacher, would have a lesson time with each grade for a few minutes. During this time homework was reviewed, questions asked and new assignments given. One always had a chance to review lessons from previous years as they were taught to the younger students.

Of course, not all lessons were learned in the classroom. One day three of the older boys decided to find out what it was like to smoke dried corn silks rolled up in notebook paper. This livened up one very dull noon-hour for Bud who had to stay in and study the spelling words he had missed. The would-be smokers had crawled under the schoolhouse to light up. The smell of smoke soon came up through the floorboards and caught the teacher's attention. Bud couldn't help but laugh as the three boys joined him in the noon-hour study hall.

On another occasion one of the boys got mad at the teacher and said an improper four-letter word to her. The next morning the head of the school board, Mr. Miller, came to the school. He calmly explained the reason for his visit, and then called the boy to the front of the room. Then Mr. Miller took off his belt and proceeded to give the boy a "good licking" as it was called in those days. Today it would be called child abuse and he would probably have lost his position on the school board and then be sued by the boy's parents. However, the boy never made that mistake again nor did Mr. Miller find it necessary to visit the school again for the rest of the year.

Then there was the Christmas tree trick that was passed on from generation to generation. The teacher would send two older boys after a Christmas tree at lunchtime. The boys would find a real nice tree and carry it to a spot near the school but still out of sight. Then they would cut a poorly shaped tree and take it to the teacher. She always tried to cover her real feelings and not hurt the boys, who knew she would not accept it. They would explain that this was the only tree close to the school, but they could go farther away if she wished. So back they went, just out of sight of the school, and had a big time throwing snowballs and sliding down the hill until school was almost out. Then they would come in bringing the beautiful tree and everyone was happy.

Valentine's Day always brought a welcome break to the long winter months. This was time for the box social at the school. The local musicians would bring their instruments and provide the entertainment. The girls would dress up in their prettiest clothes. The boys were all slicked up in their Sunday best. Then there were the beautiful boxes all wrapped as fancy as could be. Each of the girls and ladies, from youngest to the oldest, would bring their Favorite pie wrapped up real pretty. They were brought in brown paper bags, or boxes so the men and boys wouldn't be able to see which box belonged to which girl. The boxes were then auctioned off to the highest bidder one at a time. After the last box had been sold, each girl or lady would find the man or boy who had bought their box and were supposed to share the pie with them. Usually there would be a few funny match ups and sometimes one or both of the matched persons would not cooperate, but in general the persons involved were good sports and just laughed and made the best they could of the situation.

It seems like each time there was a box social you would hear someone retell the story of a joke once played on the school teacher and her boyfriend. The schoolteacher was always the first to arrive at any social at the schoolhouse. She wanted to make sure everything was neat and tidy and ready for the public. When the boxes were brought for the social they were stored in the small cloakroom in the rear of the school. There they could be closely guarded by some of the young ladies. Since the teacher arrived first, her box was put on the far end of the shelf and so would be the last one to be auctioned off. Her boyfriend who always managed to bid the highest for that particular one understood this fact. At one of the socials the girls guarding the boxes moved the teachers box to the head of the pile so it would be sold first. They put the box of the youngest little girl in its place at the end. When it came time to auction the boxes they managed to keep the teacher busy on some pretext so she wouldn't notice that her box had been taken first. In that way there would be no chance of her tipping off her boyfriend. Finally the last box was auctioned off and once again the teacher was called away. Some of the boys had been tipped off about the switch in boxes. Needless to say, her boyfriend paid a very high price for the last box only to find out that he was not to spend the rest of the evening with the teacher.

This school year was to be the best of all for Bud. He would attend nine different schools in his first eight and one half years in K through the eighth grade. The Pine Log School, met in a one room schoolhouse and taught only four grades each year, odd grades one year and even grades the next. Bud was fortunate in that he was entering the seventh grade on an odd grade year.

His sister was not so fortunate. She had just finished the seventh grade and should be entering the eighth grade. Since she was an A student they did not want to make her repeat the seventh grade. She was allowed to go to Ste. Genevieve and take a test to determine her grade level. Virginia came out with an eleventh grade level on the test and so was allowed to skip the eighth grade and go on to high school. This meant a short ride with her dad to the Clearwater store, then a forty-mile ride on the school bus over gravel roads. It also meant Bud was free to walk to his school without the bother of a sister who was not country oriented.

When school started Bud had a difficult time getting the cow in to be milked, seeing that the wood box was filled, the chickens were fed, and the water bucket made a final trip to the spring as well as the milk being put in the springhouse. He then had to walk up the road to his friends' house in time to walk to school with them. A trip that required crossing Greasy Creek several times and making the walk to school nearly twice as long. Bud would soon learn of a short cut in a more direct route but it meant walking alone much of the time.

Recesses and noon hours were Buds' favorite times of the school day. Usually the whole school, including the teacher, would join in the fun. The activities were altered from day to day so there would be games for all age groups. The older students would join in the games with the younger ones and would also include them in their own. The games would range from softball, hide-and-seek, tag, red-rover, anti-over, for the older kids, to farmer-in-the-dell, fox and the hound, drop the hanky, and hot potato for the younger ones. Since everyone usually joined in the fun it was hard to tell which games were really for which age group.

One beautiful fall day the students were pleasantly surprised to look out the window and see a large flock of geese landing in the cornfield next to the school. Bud had never seen the beautiful black, grey and white Canadian geese this close before. He could hardly wait for school to let out so they could get an even closer look. The path they always walked home on led right to the area where the geese had landed. When school finally came to an end the boys tore out of the building, over the stile, and out through the cornfield. Since the geese always posted guards they were up and away before the boys could get very close. What a thrill it was to see the big birds and to stand and watch them gradually form up into their long V in the sky. The boys watched them until they were just tiny specks in the distance, headed south. Bud had watched and listened to many flocks of the high-flying honkers in the past, but it never failed to stir him emotionally. Little did he know that he would one day follow them north to their summer breeding grounds.

The afternoon walks home were always an enjoyable part of the day. Nine or ten of the students would leave the school together. There was a lot of friendly conversation and playing around during the walk home. Once they reached the Hawthorns' place their number was reduced to four or five. At the end of Possum Hollow Bud would tell them goodbye and climb the hill towards home. The walk from there was more lonesome at times but Bud was used to being by himself a great deal and for the most part he enjoyed these quiet walks. In the winter he had to hurry along much faster in order to reach home before dark to get his chores done.

After chores and supper it was usually time for homework. This was done in the front room sitting on the daybed, which served as a couch by day and Buds' bed by night. This was done to conserve kerosene in the lamps and wood in the stove, which was the only source of heat. Since they had no electricity there was no radio or TV, bedtime, like getting up time usually came very early. Buds' father worked very hard all day at the sawmill in Coffman. In the evenings he would work around the house or in the garden or on the '36 Chevy they depended on for transportation. After supper he would usually study the Bible and other books to prepare his sermons for Sunday. His mother had few conveniences to help her with the housework. Washing clothes was done by hand with a washboard and tub. Ironing was done with heavy irons heated on the stove and was backbreaking work. Since there was no permanent press material everything had to be ironed for all four of them. Sewing and mending had to be done by hand much more slowly than by machine. Buds' sister Ginny had to ride the school bus eighty miles a day besides helping her mother in the kitchen. By nine o'clock they were usually all ready for bed.

School life was certainly different here in the hills along Greasy Creek. But it was a welcome difference to Bud. There was a feeling of closeness among the students that he had not experienced before. He could not remember seeing all the kids come to school with hands stained from hulling walnuts. In the fall he would sometimes stop long enough to pick off some persimmons for his mother. There were also trips to pick hickory nuts for the winter. Many evenings were spent cracking and digging out walnuts and hickory nuts both for cooking and eating. Many of the things done by the people along Greasy Creek were no different than things done by people who lived in the country in many parts of the state, or for that matter in most of North America. However, to Bud it was a time to remember in a special way.

Near the end of the school Bud and his family moved away from Greasy Creek to a farm near Coffman. The new home was only a mile from where his teacher lived so Bud could walk to her house and ride with her to school, so at least Bud was able to finish that year with the same teacher and students.

The teacher had to pick up other students as well and one of these required going down and up a very steep hill. The teacher was not a highly experienced driver and one day stalled her car while going up this hill.

The brakes would not hold the car unless applied very strongly. It required a very good driver to be able to take the left foot off the brake, push in the clutch, start the engine with the right foot on the starter, then move the right foot to the gas pedal and give the engine enough gas as the clutch was slowly let out, so that the car moved up the hill and nothing was torn up or the engine stalled again. The emergency brake could be used if the driver was proficient enough to coordinate the other functions just right.

To complicate matters further, the teacher could not back up using the rear-view mirror or looking over her shoulder. The car kept going backwards as she tried to start the engine so that we finally ended up in the ditch at the bottom of the hill. When her nerves settled down she was able to get the car started and we made it on to school.

The move was made because his father not only worked in Coffman, but he was now preaching every Sunday in the church in Coffman. However, life would never be quite the same as that year along Greasy Creek. He felt like he had left a part of the past behind, and moved back into the world of electricity, radios, and riding to school. He would still be attending a small one-room school next to the church to begin his eighth grade year.

In just a few months Bud was to move again, this time it would be back near the city of Farmington. He was never to live in Ste. Genevieve County again, although he would visit it a number of times throughout his lifetime. The place where they were nearly washed away in a flood would later have a bridge built over the creek. The house where he had lived would eventually be torn down. However, he was to meet Jimmy Boyd at the old baptizing hole and visit with him in his home many years later.

Jimmy Boyd & Larry Janis

The Fly and I

A poem by Larry Janis from a story in the book;
as told by Kuzin Zeke

Hit wuz a Sunday morning in thuh munth uf June
Thuh ancient pianer wuz way out uf tune.
Thuh music wuz draggin slow as cud be,
An thuh song leadin feller wuz singin off key.
They sung all the verses, hit shore did seem long,
I thought they`d ne`er reach thuh end uf thuh
song.
Thuh log church wuz stuffy, an thuh sun on my
arm
Seem tuh promise thuh air wud soon be quite
warm.

Thru thuh winder next to me, which wuz open a
crack,
I heered sum ones houn gettin hot on a track.
Quick as a wink my mind went along,
Fer tuh me thuh houns bayin wuz a pertier song.
At last in thuh distance thuh sound becum dim,
then I spied two squirrels playin out on a lim.
They uz chasin each other a-round and a-round
Sum times in ther tree, sum times on thuh
ground.
By this time thuh preacher wuz gettin into ees
text,
An I sure wern`t purpared fur whut come up next.
My friend wuz a-stairin intent as cud be,
At a fly buzzin round in thuh winder by me.
Then biden ees time an playin hit sly, ,
Behind ees lessun book whispered, catch me thet
fly.
So ith wun eye on thuh preacher an tother on
thuh glass,
I waited a spell til hit made thuh right pass.
Like thuh strike uv a rattler ith a flick uv my wrist,
I felt thuh fly buzzin inside uv my fist.
Holden still as a statue but feelin quite keen,
I glanced all about wunderin ifn I`d been seen.
All seemed tuh be clear an nobuddy knew,
Theyd be wun less fly in a minit er two.
Ever so keerful my hand opened sum,
An I retched in an got eem twixt finger an thum.
Taken keer not tuh skwish eem I handed eem ore,
Feelin quite proud how I`d handled thuh chore.

Then quick as a frogs toung when a bug passes
by,
My buddy reached ore an swatted thet fly.
Ees rolled up lessun book made a terruble sound,
An ever wun in thuh church started lookin
around.
I wuz caught with my han stickin out in thuh air,
With fly joos all ore it, I wuz filled with dispair.
Wun deacon jerked uprite, ith a sic possum grin,
Ee felt hit wuz fittin tuh add an amen.
Thuh preacher stopped preachin thuh silence
growed loud,
An ee give me a look like a dark thunder cloud.
I cud tell at a glance whut maws skowlin look sed,
Soons we git home youle be visitin thuh shed.
Hit didnt seem fair fer thuh fault wuz my friend,
But I knowed I wud catch it when church come to
an end.
I cud expect fer sum weeks tuh be sittin by maw,
Fer thuh preacher up there yuh see wuz my paw.

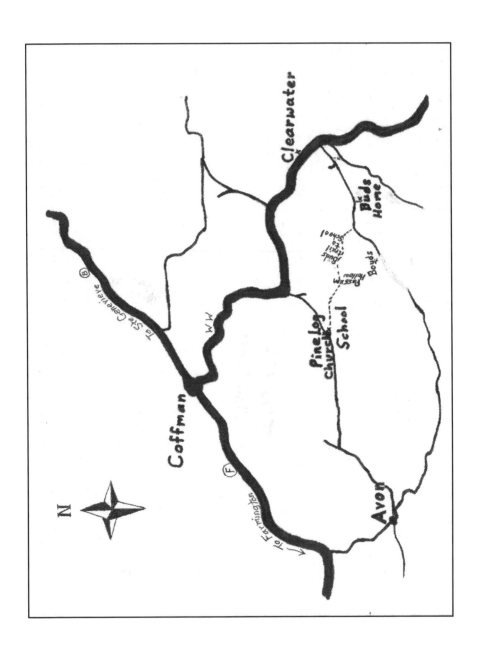

About the Author

Born in St. Louis, MO in 1937, Larry, (called Bud by his in-laws), was not to remain a city boy for long. At the age of five, after a brief ten month stay in the sunny state of California, he found himself on a dairy farm south of Farmington, MO. in St. Francois County. He was to spend most of his time on some farm until he left home at the age of 17 to begin his world travels.

However, one of those farms would be more memorable than the others. That was the year he would be in the 7th grade and live along Greasy Creek. Strangely enough this move would take him into Ste. Genevieve county as his Great ... Grandfather had done back in the 1700's when the city of Ste. Genevieve was founded and he became the proprietor of the first inn west of the Mississippi River. This was a fact of history that Larry would not be aware of until many years later as he had little interest in education prior to becoming a man.

At 17 Larry entered the military, again as his Great ... Grandfather had done when he joined with

George Rogers Clark's forces and became the flag bearer in the capture of Fort Vincennes in Indiana during the Revolutionary War, On his second tour of duty, (the Army first then the Air Force), Larry finally made a belated start on his formal education. It would culminate many years later with a masters degree in, of all things, educational administration. Along the way he would not only accumulate some 240 semester hours of formal education, but also many informal programs such as: carpentry, heavy equipment operation, truck driving, long range radar repair, electronics, emergency medical training, pilot's license, (bush flying in Alaska), IBM office products repair, auto-body repair, and repelling instructor.

Larry, with his late wife Patsy, daughter Susan and their German Shepherd, Ginger, moved to Alaska in 1972 where he would teach a number of things, including 7th grade science. A far cry from his time spent along Greasy Creek as a boy who hated school. To make it even more of an unlikely situation he would be teaching in a small country town called Wasilla. You may have already guessed the next part of this strange situation. In 1977 one of his students was to be a young lady by the name of Sarah Heath who would become the first female governor of Alaska and later the first female to run for vice president for the Republican Party. A teacher never knows what the future holds for their students.

Alaska was to hold even more that would affect Larry's life. Due to circumstances both within and beyond his control, (his home caught on fire), he would realize a lifelong dream of becoming a pilot. Thanks to several missionary pilots that he worked with he was able to buy a 1934 Taylorcraft. A small 65-horsepower airplane that in the right hands made a very nice bush plane. Larry's instructor happened to have one of these planes and was an excellent pilot. Due to his background in farm work and later in the military his work with heavy equipment and trucks of various sizes he was able to pick up the ability to fly his T-cart into and out of some very small places.

Larry also became acquainted with an entertainer by the name of Larry Beck who quoted Robert Service poetry. He was so impressed with the performances of this sourdough that he wanted to imitate what Larry Beck was doing but in a little different way. During long drives and flights the character of Kuzin Zeke gradually took shape. Instead of a sourdough miner, Kuzin Zeke became a make believe hillbilly from an obscure place, known as Greasy Creek. This required a lot of work in changing the pronunciation of many words from the poems he quoted as well as new ones he wrote. He never did this for money but did enough to become known as Zeke to many of his friends.

Larry also continued his work in black-light chalk art. With his wife Patsy being an excellent pianist and his daughter Susan becoming old enough (4 years old) and with her mothers training, good enough to become a soloist they began a real family ministry that would continue for many years. Along with his chalk art Larry also worked to improve his artistic talents with various mediums, from painting gold pans and ceramics in Alaska to pictures for fund-raisers in St. Louis, or illustrations for books and teaching aids, he spent much of his spare time doing art work. During his time in Alaska, Larry was the recipient of a government mini-grant to design and build a one-of-a-kind historic totem pole for the Matanuska-Susitna Valley. This led him to visit the kennels of Joe Redington, father of the Iditarod Trail dog sled race. Also the ghost town of Iditarod and the gold mining area around Flat where the Guggenheim family fortune was made.

In 1980 Larry and his family moved back to St Louis where he taught in a Christian school for 15 years. After 2 heart attacks,(one while hiking in the Grand Canyon), and a quadruple bypass he retired from teaching.

The next 15 years were spent doing maintenance work at Tower Grove Baptist Church and school before retireing for the fourth and final time.

Beginning at the age of 18 Larry was transferred to France by the US Army. This began his travels that would result in his visiting 23 countries. After a second tour of duty, this time in the US Air Force in England, Larry would marry Patsy Rucker in St. Louis and continue his travels. They would visit all 49 of the continental states and all but one of the Canadian Provinces, (this one would later be split into two). Larry loved to drive and his wife loved to travel so together with Susan and one of their four German Shepherds they drove as far north as Deadhorse, Alaska on the Arctic Ocean to Goosebay, Labrador in Canada.

Larry's driving experiences would progress from horses along Greasy Creek, to camels in the Sahara Desert, from tractors of various types on farms in Missouri, to earth movers in France plus military vehicles from jeeps to eighteen-wheelers. And finally to flying over the mountains and through the passes of the Alaska Range.

He has taken ferries across several of Missouri's rivers to those along the Pacific coast of the US and Canada, and the Atlantic coast from the US to various Canadian Provinces. Larry has also sailed across the Atlantic and the Mediterranean, encountering a hurricane along the way.

From 115° in Death Valley to the minus 55° in the banana belt of Alaska. From beneath the ocean in the coal mines of St. Johns, Nova Scotia to the hard rock gold mines in the mountains of Hatchers' Pass near Wasilla, Alaska. From the salty depths of the Dead Sea in Jordan to the pure snows of the Saint Bernard pass in the Alps. From the ancient monastery carved into the red rock high above the rose-red city of Petra to the modern creation museum in Kentucky. The author as a boy studying a number of newly hatched catfish in one of many pools of water in Greasy Creek could never have imagined what God had in store for him in the future. Every area of learning that Bud would later be involved in became useful at one time or another in his life. As a final word of advice to the readers of this little book I would suggest that each one would learn all they could and then place their life in God's hands and just see where He will lead you. Proverbs 3:5-6 gives us the directions if we will just follow them.

Notes

Notes

Notes

Notes

Notes

Notes

Notes